# Towards Understanding Tauheed

## Reflections on Islamic Monotheism

by

### Shaikh Muhammad Ahmad Bashmeel

*Translation from Arabic by*
*Abdul-Khaliq Nadwi & M.S. Kayani*

*Revised and Edited by*
*Dr Ashraf Muhammad*

Published by: AR-RAQEEM PUBLICATIONS.
P.O Box 9688, London N22 4WA, UK.

First published 1995/1416 AH

British Library Cataloguing in Publication Data


ISBN: 1 900598 00 0


A catalogue record for this book is available from the British Library.


Typeset and design by: AR-RAQEEM PUBLICATIONS


Printed in Great Britain by
Whitstable Litho Printers Ltd., Whitstable, Kent.

# PREFACE

## In the Name of Allah the Beneficent the Merciful

May Allah send His Peace and Blessings on the last of the Prophets and Messengers, Muhammad.

The sole purpose for which Allah - the Most High - has brought all beings into existence and sent His messengers to them is that all of them should worship Him alone:

﴿ وَما خَلَقْتُ الْجِنَّ والإِنسَ إِلَّا لِيَعْبُدون ﴾ الذاريات: ٥٦

*I have not created Jinns and human beings but to worship Me.*
*[Adh-Dhariyat, 51: 56]*

It is a sad fact that the masses of ignorant Muslims do not know the real meaning of *'ibadah* (worship); they address their worship (unknowingly) to other than Allah, thereby committing a kind of *shirk* (associating partners with Allah), which would drive a person right out of Islam.

They turn in awe and submission to the graves of prophets and righteous people, invoking them, seeking their help, making vows and offering sacrifices to them. They go round their graves, shrines and sarcophaguses (as an act of exaltation) just as they would go round the holy Ka'bah performing *tawaf*. **This is nothing but worship,** even though

3

they may call it *'tabarruk'* (seeking blessings) or *'tawassul'* (seeking their intercession, or supplicating Allah through them as intermediaries).

These common Muslims may be committing this kind of *shirk* out of ignorance and lack of understanding of the meaning of *'ibadah*; if so, they might have some excuse on account of their ignorance. But what excuse do the scholars of eminence who understand the real meaning of *'ibadah* have? Deep in their hearts, they know that what these lay people are doing is a form of the 'greater *shirk'*, which drives who commits it out of Islam. They issue *fatwas* stating that different forms of *shirk* (of word, belief and action) committed by these ignorant people are nothing but a desirable kind of *tawassul* and an expression of reverence for prophets and righteous people.

Furthermore, these scholars themselves commit acts of *shirk* on such occasions as birthdays of prophets and saints and other invented anniversaries, thus allowing *shirk* to take root in the hearts of the common people, who regard them as their **role models**.

Such scholars, who hide the truth and encourage *kufr* (unbelief, disacknowledgment or denial), have no fear of Allah. For a trivial price or high status, soon to vanish, they commit these sins against themselves and against lay people. It is these scholars who have strayed from the right path and lead others astray.

**Dear reader,**

Having realised with great dismay that forms of greater *shirk* are rife throughout the Muslim World, I turned to

4

Allah seeking His support and guidance and putting my trust in Him. I wrote this book on *tauheed* (monotheism) entitled *Towards Understanding Tauheed* (Reflections on Islamic Monotheism).

I pray that Allah may accept this modest work, and make it a source of guidance for His servants who have gone astray, knowingly or unknowingly. It is a humble effort on my part to bring those whom Allah wishes into the light of *tauheed* from the darkness of *shirk*.

**Allah is the best of helpers and the best of protectors.**

**Shaikh Muhammad Ahmad Bashmeel**

> "The ties of Islam will be broken one after the other when there are people born and brought up in Islam, who do not know what jahiliyah* is."

## 'Umar ibn Al-Khattab

* The term *jahiliyah* denotes the period of Arabian paganism before the advent of the Prophet Muhammad (peace be upon him) or the state of pagan ignorance characteristic of that period; the latter meaning is intended here.

He[1] was a very religious man, noted for his courteousness and kindly disposition, yet extremely frank. We have always seen eye to eye, but there is one issue over which we had to differ: the practice of appealing to the dead for intercession, invoking them, imploring their aid instead of Allah's, and making sacrifices and vows to them. We used to argue about it and I gathered from his arguments that he, like many others, was of the opinion that all such practices were at least permissible, if not recommendable.

One day he said to me, "You know that I have never turned to anyone other than Allah, and I have never sought to advance myself in His favour by any means other than my own deeds."

"I know that", I said; "In fact, this is what makes me think highly of you and raises my hopes about you." "A sensible man like yourself", I added, "should not fail to see the wrongness of such follies committed by gullible people who have fallen victim to the custodians of graves and the opportunists who have commercialized tombs and mausoleums."

## Is supplicating dead prophets and righteous people a form of *kufr*?

He said, "But, as I have told you several times before, I can't quite understand why supplicating the dead, especially prophets, righteous people or *auliya'* (those who are considered to be close to Allah by virtue of their devotion), should be regarded as a form of *shirk* which drives who commits it out of the fold of Islam. How could that be so when those who turn to the dead for help or intercession do not ascribe to them any power to do harm or good, to create or originate, to give life or death; nor do they ascribe to them any other powers possessed only by Allah?"

---

*1- This book is based on a dialogue between the author and a friend of his.*

We often had discussions about the subject along these lines, though they were mostly brief and superficial, but neither of us could convince the other.

Then one day he asked me, "Would you like to discuss this issue frankly? Let's this time discuss it from all aspects, but with one condition: that we do so dispassionately; people can only go astray when they are gripped by emotions and driven by desires and inclinations."

I said, "To tell you the truth, I've been eagerly waiting for this moment for so long; I'm anxious to point out some hidden and rather obscure aspects which could be the cause of your confusion and uncertainty. So I'd be delighted to discuss this issue with you in depth."

"Great!", he enthused; "Now, what is your exact position on this matter? What conclusive evidence have you got for regarding those who follow this practice - that is who supplicate the dead, seek the aid of prophets and righteous people, or make offerings and vows to them - as *kuffar* (disbelievers) who have come out of the fold of Islam?"

"Our position is in conformity with the Holy Qur'an.", I replied. "It is not just a point of view we adopted or a theory we made up. Rather, it is simply an extension of the verdict of the Eternal Book to which no falsehood can ever attain, neither overtly nor covertly. So it is the Holy Qur'an, not us, that has denounced those grave-worshippers as *kuffar*, and regarded their deeds as *shirk* ."

He said in his usual calmness, "There is no need to repeat these unqualified statements; I've become only too familiar with them. To my mind, they are nothing but a claim , and a claim without evidence is not acceptable. So where is your detailed convincing proof?! The matter is far greater and more serious than simply making such unqualified, unsubstantiated statements. By accusing Muslims of being *kuffar,* so readily and carelessly, you have plunged Muslims into serious *fitnah* (discord and division), from which they are still suffering."

## Misrepresentations by grave-worshippers

"You are still under the influence of widespread misleading propaganda", I said. "It has impaired your thinking and given rise to your misconceptions about us.

"Anyway, you are free to describe what we have done - and continue to do - as *fitnah*, rashness impetuousness, or whatever you may wish to call it. It does not change the plain truth: that we have contemplated the Book of Allah as He commanded us to, and found that Allah's description of the earlier polytheists fits exactly those grave-worshippers, who supplicate the dead, implore their help and make vows and offerings to them besides Allah.

"So we did not hesitate to warn and explain, nor were we afraid anybody when we disclosed our conclusions. We said it all loud and clear to the faces of those who are too arrogant and stubborn to admit the truth. We did not care whether this would make anybody pleased or displeased with us. People's pleasure or displeasure could never be the yardstick of truth or falsehood."

## Refuting the false arguments of polytheists and grave-worshippers

"Here is the evidence for what we are asserting out of obedience to Allah. Firstly, you maintain that, supplicating the dead, asking for their help and support, making offerings and vows to them in the hope of winning their favour, or for the

9

sake of their mediation or intercession with Allah, is neither *shirk* nor *kufr* so long as one believes in the divinity of Allah and holds that He alone, *subhanahu wa ta'ala*, is the Creator, the Provider and the Giver of life and death, and that those who are invoked besides Him for support can do neither good nor harm to themselves.

"But actually this is an incorrect theory and a false analysis which completely contradicts the very foundations of Islam. You will come to see this clearly in due course *insha'allah*.

## The real nature of the conflict between the prophets and the polytheists

"If you study the conflicts that arose between the prophets (especially our Prophet Muhammad, peace be upon him) and the earlier polytheists, you will find that they did not result from those polytheists's denial of the existence of Allah or their disbelief in Him. Nor were these conflicts caused by their refusal to accept that Allah Almighty has dominion over everything, or their belief that the idols they worshipped besides Allah shared His power to bring benefit or avert harm. Nothing of the kind occurred to those polytheists, and none of them had any such beliefs."

## The Polytheists' belief in Allah

"Those polytheists unshakeably believed in the existence of Allah. They also had an absolute faith in His Oneness as the only Creator and Provider. In other words, they believed that Allah was their Lord and the Lord of all creation; that the so-called gods and prophets to whom they addressed their supplications were nothing more than servants and creatures of Allah, who did not even have the power to avert harm from,

10

or bring benefit to, themselves; and that the power to harm and benefit and give life and death vested only in Allah. None of His creatures could share this power or oppose it.

"This is how the earlier polytheists believed in Allah and had a pure faith in His unshared *rububiyah* (His Lordship: the fact that He is the Lord, Creator and Provider); a faith that is not matched by present-day grave-worshippers, who would only in hardship appeal to some dead righteous people buried in mausoleums for help and protection.

"By contrast, the earlier polytheists did not pray to their gods and goddesses at times of calamity and distress, but rather they would resort to Allah alone, associating nothing and no one with Him."

At this point my friend was beginning to lose his calmness; "That's absurd! How could it be?", he protested.

### Tauheed of Abu Jahl and Abu Lahab[2]

"Abu Jahl and Abu Lahab, and other earlier polytheists like them, all believed in Allah.", I replied. "As far as *rububiyah* is concerned, they were monotheists; they believed that Allah was the One and Only Creator, Provider, Giver of life and death, Owner of the power to harm and benefit. They associated no partners with Him in this respect."

"Very strange! Very strange indeed!", my friend exclaimed; "are you seriously suggesting that Abu Jahl and Abu Lahab had a stronger and more genuine belief in Allah and His

---

2 - *Two well-known polytheists who lived at the time of the Prophet (peace be upon him) and were extremely opposed to Islam*

Oneness than those Muslims who declare that there is no god but Allah and that Muhammad is His Messenger?! You must be out of your mind! How could you have the audacity to say such a thing! In fact, it is such serious and exaggerated assertions that have made people like you antagonize millions of Muslims throughout the world."

"It is neither strange nor astonishing", I replied. "Rather, it is the truth, which you will come to realize and acknowledge, *insha'allah*, when the facts and proofs are laid out clearly in front of you. Only then will you be able to purge your mind of the fallacies you regard as valid arguments and proofs."

## Proof of the earlier polytheists' belief in Allah and His Oneness

He reacted angrily saying: "All right! Let's hear your so-called 'proof'. If it is true, as you claim, that the earlier polytheists had such a belief in Allah, what is meant by the *shirk* which He attributed to them? Why did Allah condemn them to an eternal hell fire, having made it permissible to kill them and confiscate their property, and having commanded His prophet (peace be upon him) to fight them?"

"The evidence stems from nothing but the Holy Qur'an", I replied; "it is in this Eternal Scripture, which you and millions of Muslims who share your view recite day and night, worshipping Allah, but without pondering over its meaning or grasping its message."

## Confession of the earlier polytheists that Allah alone is the Creator, Provider, and Giver of life and death

"Allah Almighty has emphasized the earlier polytheists' belief in Him as the Creator, Provider, the One Who gives life and death, and the One Who has the power to harm and benefit. Addressing His Prophet (peace be upon him) about those polytheists, Allah *subhanahu wa ta'ala*, said:

﴿ وَلَئِن سَأَلْتَهُم مَن خَلَقَ السَّمَاوَاتِ والأرْضَ وَسَخَّرَ الشَّمْسَ وَالْقَمَرَ لَيَقُولُنَّ الله فَأَنَّى يُؤْفَكُون ﴾ العنكبوت: ٦١

*If indeed you ask them who has created the heavens and earth and subjected the sun and the moon (to His Law), they will certainly reply, "Allah." How are they then deluded away (from the truth)? [Al-'Ankabut, 29: 61]*

﴿ وَلَئِن سَأَلْتَهُم مَن نَزَّلَ مِنَ السَّمَاءِ مَاءً فَأَحْيَا بِهِ الأرْضَ مِن بَعْدِ مَوْتِهَا لَيَقُولُنَّ الله قُلِ الْحَمْدُ لله بَلْ أَكْثَرُهُمْ لايَعْقِلُون ﴾ العنكبوت: ٦٣

*And if indeed you ask them who it is that sends down rain from the sky and gives life therewith to the earth after its death, they will certainly reply, "Allah!" Say, "Praise be to Allah!" But most of them understand not. [Al-'Ankabut, 29: 63]*

﴿ قُل لِمَنِ الأرْضُ وَمَن فِيهَا إِن كُنتُم تَعْلَمُونَ * سَيَقُولُونَ لله قُل أَفَلَا تَذَكَّرُون * قُل مَن رَبُّ السَّمَاوَاتِ السَّبْعِ وَرَبُّ الْعَرْشِ الْعَظِيمِ * سَيَقُولُون لله قُل أَفَلَا تَتَّقُون * قُل مَن بِيَدِهِ مَلَكُوتُ كُلِّ شَيْءٍ وَهُوَ يُجِيرُ وَلا يُجَارُ عَلَيْهِ إِن كُنتُم تَعْلَمُونَ * سَيَقُولُونَ لله قُل فَأَنَّى تُسْحَرُون ﴾

المؤمنون: ٨٤ – ٨٩

*Say, "To whom belong the earth and all beings therein? (Say) if you know!" They will say, "To Allah!" Say, "Yet will you not receive admonition?" Say, "Who is the Lord of the seven*

*heavens, and the Lord of the Mighty Throne?" They will say,*
*"They belong to Allah." Say: "Will you not then fear?" Say,*
*"in Whose Hands is the sovereignty of all things, and Who is it*
*that protects while there is no protection against Him? (Say) if*
*you know. They will say: "(It belongs) to Allah." Say: "Then*
*how are you deluded?"*
*[Al-Mu'minun, 23: 84 - 89]*

﴿ قُل مَن يَرْزُقُكُم مِنَ السَّماءِ والأرضِ أم مَن يَمْلِكُ السَّمْعَ والأَبْصَارَ وَمَن يُخْرِجُ الْحَيَّ مِن الْمَيِّتِ وَيُخْرِجُ الْمَيِّتَ مِنَ الْحَيِّ وَمَن يُدَبِّرُ الأمْرَ فَسَيَقُولُونَ اللهُ فَقُلْ أفَلا تَتَّقُون ﴾ يونس: ٣١

*Say, "Who is it that sustains you (in life) from the sky and from*
*the earth? Or who is it that has power over hearing and sight?*
*And who is it that brings out the living from the dead and the*
*dead from the living? And who is that rules and regulates all*
*affairs?" They will soon say, "Allah". Say: "Will you not then*
*show piety to (Him)?" [Yunus, 10: 31]*

"These clear verses", I went on, "represent our incontestable evidence that the earlier polytheists did not deny the existence of Allah, nor did they believe He had partners running with Him the affairs of His Kingdom. Rather, they had an absolute belief that there was only one Lord: Allah.

"The verses I have just quoted prove beyond a shadow of doubt that they did not turn to their alleged gods in the hope that they would prolong life, ward off death, or bring rain.

"They would never turn to their so-called gods to bring them happiness or to put an end to their hardship. After all, how could they do so when they firmly believed that only Allah, the Master and Sovereign of everything, had the power to grant

14

them what they were asking for, as it is clear from the verses I have just quoted.

"Given this conclusive evidence, it is clearly wrong to argue -as you do- that those who invoke anything or anyone other than Allah would only be regarded as polytheists if they believed that whatever they invoked was capable, as Allah is, of causing harm and bringing benefit. This condition on the definition of *shirk* is evidently untenable.

"If your condition and claim were Islamically valid, Allah would not have ascribed *shirk* to Abu Lahab, Abu Jahl and their party; the condition you insist on is met in their case as well, since they did not believe that what they used to invoke besides Allah shared His power to bring about harm or benefit. This fact has been made abundantly clear in the verses I quoted from the Qur'an."

**The earlier polytheists had a greater faith than the polytheists of our time!**

"The proof that the earlier polytheists' faith in Allah and His oneness was stronger than that of present-day grave-worshippers can also be found in the Qur'an, the everlasting treasure and ever-shining light. Referring to those polytheists, Allah Almighty says in the Qur'an:

﴿ فَإِذَا رَكِبُوا فِي الْفُلْكِ دَعَوُا اللهَ مُخْلِصِينَ لَهُ الدِّينَ فَلَمَّا نَجَّاهُمْ إِلَى الْبَرِّ إِذَا هُمْ يُشْرِكُونَ ﴾ العنكبوت: ٦٥

*When they embark on a boat, they call on Allah making their devotion sincerely (and exclusively) to Him; but as soon as He has brought them safe to land they give a share (of their worship to others) ! [Al-'Ankabut, 29: 65]*

﴿ وَإِذَا مَسَّكُمُ الضُّرُّ فِي البَحْرِ ضَلَّ مَن تَدْعُونَ إِلَّا إِيَّاهُ فَلَمَّا نَجَّاكُم إِلَى البَرِّ
أَعْرَضْتُم وَكَانَ الإِنسَانُ كَفُوراً ﴾ الإِسراء: ٦٧

*When distress seizes you at sea, those that you call upon -besides*
*Himself- leave you in the lurch! But when He brings you back*
*safe to land, you turn away (from Him). Most ungrateful is*
*man! [Al- Isra', 17: 67]*

﴿ قُل مَن يُنَجِّيكُم مِن ظُلُمَاتِ البَرِّ والبَحْرِ تَدْعُونَهُ تَضَرُّعاً وَخُفْيَةً لَئِن أَنجَانَا مِن
هَذِهِ لَنَكُونَنَّ مِنَ الشَّاكِرِينَ * قُل اللهُ يُنَجِّيكُم مِنهَا وَمِن كُلِّ كَرْبٍ ثُمَّ أَنتُم
تُشرِكُونَ ﴾ الإنعام: ٦٣ – ٦٤

*Say: "Who is it that delivers you from the dark recesses of land*
*and sea, when you call upon Him in humility and in secret: 'If He*
*only delivers us from these (dangers), (we vow) we shall truly*
*show our gratitude'? Say: "It is Allah that delivers you from*
*these and all (other) distresses: and yet you worship false gods!"*
*[Al-An'am, 6: 63-64]*

"These verses show that when the earlier polytheists
encountered any dangers on a sea voyage, and expected the
worse to happen to them, they would then forget their false
gods and whatever they idolized besides Allah, and would no
longer believe in them. They would turn to Allah with sincere
devotion, invoking Him, pinning all their hopes on Him and
Him alone.

"This they would do in the full conviction that whoever and
whatever they used to turn to besides Allah were too
insignificant and too weak to offer them any help in their
predicament. They were in no doubt that those false gods

would not be able to hear their prayers, let alone answer them.

"Suddenly at this critical moment, the veil of fallacies and distortions that blinds them is torn apart and the truth shines through: none but Allah could be turned to at such difficult moments."

**How the earlier polytheists turned to their Lord in hardships forgetting their false gods.**

"So they would turn to Allah alone in sincere devotion, calling upon Him and invoking His help. They would disregard whoever and whatever they idolized besides Him at times of prosperity out of firm conviction that He alone, *subhanahu wa ta'ala*, could save them from drowning. They would offer sincere devotion to Allah so long as they were in danger. But once they were brought safely to shore, they would revert to the old practices of their forefathers, namely associating partners with Allah in their supplications, sacrifices and vows. It is for this reason that Allah described the actions of those people after they are brought to safety with the verb *'yushrikun'* (i.e. commit *shirk* or associate others with Him in worship):

﴿ ... فَلَمَّا نَجَّاهُم إِلَى البَرِّ إِذَا هُم يُشرِكُونَ ﴾ العنكبوت: ٦٥

*... But as soon as He has brought them safe to land, they give a share (of their worship to others)! [Al-'Ankabut, 29: 65]*

"This shows how the earlier polytheists were sincerely devoted to Allah and invoked none but Him, whenever they found themselves in difficulty or danger."

17

**How the polytheists of our time forget their Lord and turn to their *auliya'* in hardship**

"Unlike the earlier polytheists, the polytheists of our time, that is the grave-worshippers, would only turn to Allah while they are leading a life of ease and comfort. But when they are in difficulty or distress, they forget Allah and turn instead to some dead people whom they regard as protectors. They would deify them by invoking their help and making vows and sacrifices to them in fear, hope and humility.

"Only at times of hardship and distress would you hear the names of Al-Badawi, Al-Jilani, Al-Rifa'i, At-Tijani, Al-'Idrus, ibn 'Isa and other so-called *auliya'*, being called out with such fervour and devotion.

"Now, if such grave-worshippers happened to be on board a ship in a stormy sea, they would not turn to Allah, but rather to their *auliya'*. They would readily seek their help and invoke their protection; you would hear them calling out their names in utter humility and submissiveness, 'Help! O Badawi, O Jilani, O Rifa'i, ...'. You would see them imploring their imaginary protectors as if they were there with them.

"And if you could see how they would anxiously and submissively vie with one another to make vows to those dead people and offer sacrifices to them, if they saved them from drowning, only then would you realize how contemptible and degrading is such a state of *shirk* and *kufr* which strips man of his dignity and brings him down from the level of a human being who possesses the power of reasoning to a level lower than that of grazing cattle.

"What could be more despicable and degrading for a man than him turning away from his Creator and Sustainer, from his

Lord who is ever-watchful of him, only to seek help and protection from decaying bones, which could not even protect themselves or the flesh that once covered them against the attacking worms; and to beg these bones to save him from drowning?! Allah has spoken the truth when He said,

$$
﴿ وَمَن أَضَلُّ مِمَّن يَدْعُوا مِن دُونِ اللهِ مَن لا يَسْتَجِيبُ لَهُ إِلَى يَوْمِ القِيَامَةِ وَهُم عَن دُعَائِهِم غَافِلُونَ ﴾ الأحقاف: ٥
$$

*And who is more astray than one who invoke, besides Allah, such as will not answer him to the Day of Judgement, and are not even conscious of being invoked? [Al-Ahqaf, 46: 5]*

"I have witnessed so many of these follies and practices of *shirk* reminiscent of *jahiliyah,* and I was greatly troubled and distressed by what I saw."

## Confrontation with some grave-worshippers on a stormy sea journey

"I saw a lot of those people fervently invoking the dead when we were sailing across the red sea some 25 years ago. We were over 80 passengers on board a sailing boat. Suddenly, we were overtaken by a storm and the huge waves almost engulfed our boat. At times, the boat would sink between the waves as though it was going to settle on the bottom of the sea ; but then it would bounce up again with the waves as if it was being thrown up in the air.

"At this critical moment, the grave-worshippers started crying out for help and protection. Their supplications were not addressed to Allah, Who is Omnipotent and Omnipresent, but rather to the dead, who are powerless to do anything for them.

"In fear and humility, they turned to Shaikh Sa'id ibn 'Isa - may Allah have mercy on him - who died over 600 years ago. Driven by terror and hope, they cried out his name begging him for help, 'O ibn 'Isa! help! Oh pillar of faith! Deliver us from this predicament'. They were competing with one another in making vows and pledging to offer sacrifices at his grave if they were saved, as if it was him, and not Allah Almighty, who had their destiny in his hands!"

## The grave-worshippers were about to throw me in the sea

"Young as I was at the time, I tried to convince them that in a situation like the one we were facing a Muslim should only turn to Allah. I urged them in all sincerity and compassion to address their supplication and devotion exclusively to Allah, and refrain from begging Shaikh ibn 'Isa since he had no power over this matter; he could not hear their supplications let alone answer them! They flew into a rage and called me *'wahhabi'.*[3] They were even about to throw me into the sea, but Allah protected me from them by making some people on board, who concealed their faith, intervene on my behalf.

"The storm subsided and we were saved, by the help and grace of Allah alone, and obviously not thanks to ibn 'Isa. Then some of these grave-worshippers came up to me  and started to reproach me and warn me against disbelieving in the power of *auliya'.* They maintained that we were all indebted to those saintly people for our safety, and that if it had not been for the presence of the *'qutb'* (the 'pillar of faith' ibn 'Isa) at such a critical moment, all of us would be by now food for the fish."

---

3 - *A term related to the great Muslim scholar Muhammad ibn Abdul Wahhab (1703 - 1792) who strove to purge Islam of innovations and bring Muslim back to pure faith*

## Myth of the presence of *auliya'* at times of distress

"It pained me to hear them utter those words which were tantamount to unequivocal *kufr*, so I said to them, 'you are wronging yourselves and lying about Shaikh ibn 'Isa, may Allah have mercy on his soul. This dead Shaikh could not have heard your supplications, let alone answer them or be here to deliver you from the storm. Are you out of your minds?! Instead of turning to Allah, you invoke the help of a dead man! Allah has stated in the Qur'an that the dead cannot hear:

﴿ إِنَّكَ لَا تُسْمِعُ المَوْتَى وَلَا تُسْمِعُ الصُّمَّ الدُّعَاءَ إِذَا وَلَّوْا مُدْبِرِينَ ﴾ النمل: ٨٠

*Truly you cannot cause the dead to listen nor can you cause the deaf to hear the call (especially) when they turn back in retreat.*
*[An-Naml, 27: 80]*

﴿ وَمَا يَسْتَوِي الأَحْيَاءُ وَلَا الأَمْوَاتُ إِنَّ الله يُسْمِعُ مَن يَشَاءُ وَمَا أنتَ بِمُسْمِعِ مَن فِي الْقُبُورِ ﴾ فاطر: ٢٢

*Nor are alike those that are living and those that are dead. Allah can make any that He wills to hear; but you cannot make those to hear who are (buried) in grave[4].*
*[Fatir, 35: 22]*

---

4 - *This is a universal immutable law, namely that the dead do not hear except in certain special cases where there is evidence to the contrary; this exception, however, does not invalidate the general rule. What evidence do those grave-worshippers have to support their claim that their dead auliya' could hear them? Has it been stated anywhere in the Qur'an that Allah has conferred upon a particular dead person the exceptional power to hear people calling him wherever they are? And even if we assume for argument's sake that the dead do hear them, has Allah granted those people permission to turn to the dead, instead of turning to Him, and invoke their help and protection? Has He told them that the dead have been empowered to answer their calls and save them when requested to do so? These questions have never been answered convincingly by grave-worshippers, and they will remain unanswered until the Day of Reckoning.*

21

'On account of your ignorance of Allah's laws and your reluctance to study His book, you have committed these stupidities; you have turned away from Allah, the Omnipotent, the All-hearing, the All-seeing, and sought help instead from the powerless dead who are unaware of you; who can neither hear nor see you.

'It was neither ibn 'Isa nor anybody else that saw us through the storm. It was none but Allah Almighty who saved us by His grace. He did not do it because you implored a righteous man or appealed to a prophet. None of these righteous people or prophets was with us at that critical moment; there was only Allah, the One , the Absolute, who enables us to travel on land and sea.

'We do not deny that Allah is above all and has all power in His hand', one of them conceded philosophically. 'But this is an old piece of casuistry which was also used by the earlier polytheists', I hastened to reply; 'your actions contradict your words; if you genuinely believed in what you have just said, you would not have turned away from the Lord, the Creator, the Almighty, at a time of difficulty and distress, to an insignificant dead creature. By so doing, you in fact proved to have less faith in Allah than the earlier polytheists who would turn to Him alone with sincere devotion when in need, difficulty or distress, as He described them in the Qur'an.'

## How Satan appears to the grave-worshippers as one of their so-called *auliya'*

'The fact of the matter is that you hate the *auliya'* and do not believe in their miracles; that is why Allah deprived you of the

22

delight of seeing what we saw at that critical moment', argued another complacently, as if he refuted me.

'Who told you I hate them or deny their miracles?', I asked; 'have you ever heard me insult any of the *auliya'* or make a disparaging remark about any righteous person? Or have you heard me reject any proven miracles, reported in the Qur'an or Sunnah, which Allah has empowered one of His close devotees to perform?

'Have you heard me, for instance, reject the miracles of the people of the cave, who were stranded inside a cave whose entrance had been blocked by a huge rock, and then the rock was miraculously lifted out of its place by the grace of Allah? Or have I denied that Abu Bakr, 'Umar, 'Uthman, 'Ali or other companions of the Prophet (peace be upon him) were counted among Allah's *auliya'* who had been promised paradise, as reported in the *Hadith*? Or is it perhaps the oft-repeated accusation levelled against whoever refuses to go along with your absurdities or vouch for your myths?

'But do tell me', I urged him, 'what is that delightful scene which Allah has deprived me of watching, and which you and your friends here were privileged to witness when the ship was about to sink?'

'We saw the great *qutb*, Shaikh Sa'id ibn 'Isa appear like a torch of light holding on to the mast.', he replied. 'He turned to the sea and asked it to calm down, which it did; so we were saved with the blessing of the great *qutb*.'

'Had you ever before seen Shaikh Sa'id ibn 'Isa Al-'Amudi, who died more than 600 years ago?', I asked derisively.

'Of course not!'

'How do you know then that whoever you saw at the top of the mast giving orders to the sea to become calm was Shaikh Sa'id ibn 'Isa Al-'Amudi when you had never seen him before?! Have you received any revelation from Heaven assuring you that whatever or whoever you saw (assuming you did see something) was Shaikh Sa'id ibn 'Isa?' At this point he was perplexed and did not reply.

### In a frenzy of gloom he imagined ibn 'Isa was present with him

I said to him, 'In fact you saw neither ibn 'Isa nor anyone else for that matter at the mast, but in your fear and frenzy your imagination ran amuck and (with a little help from the devil) made you believe that what you saw was ibn 'Isa in order to plunge you deeper and deeper in your error and lead you further astray in the wilderness of your ignorance.'

He responded to me in a strange manner; he started to shout angrily, which brought our conversation to an end: '*Wahhabi!* Blasphemer! Disbeliever!' This is the final weapon these people resort to when confronted with a cogent argument or a conclusive proof.

Having narrated this story, I asked my friend, "Now, what do you think? Is it not enough to convince you that the faith and trust of the earlier polytheists in their Lord at times of hardship was far stronger than the grave-worshippers' faith in Allah, *subhanahu wata'ala*?"

### Fallacies of the grave-worshippers

He said, "You are being very harsh on these people when you accuse them of committing *shirk,* and say that their faith in Allah and belief in His Oneness is weaker than that of the earlier polytheists. You know very well that when these people you call 'grave-worshippers' cried out the name of ibn 'Isa invoking his help in that crisis, they did not do so because of any lack of trust in Allah or because they believed that ibn 'Isa or anyone else they called upon had the powers to help them travel in land and sea, or that they were there present with them listening to their cries and responding to them as Allah *subhanahu wa ta'ala* can do.

"In fact, they did so because they believed that Allah would rescue them by the intervention of these righteous people. They cried out their names at that difficult time only because they believed that these righteous people had attained an exalted position in Allah's sight, and that for their sake Allah would deliver those in distress as a mark of honouring His friends who suffer neither grief nor sorrow."

"This is an old fallacy that has been repeated over and over", I said. "A sensible person with any respect for his intellect could not accept it for a number of reasons:

"If these grave-worshippers did not believe that some dead righteous people were present with them in times of joy and adversity and listened to their supplications and responded to them, and had the power to save them, they would not have invoked their help with such devotion and humility like a helpless wretch begging the Almighty Who has power over all things. If they truly did not believe this, they would not make vows to them nor pledge to make offerings to them in the hope that they would save them from drowning; indeed, they would not fulfil their vows out of fear and hope.

"Would any sensible person call upon someone who he knows could neither hear nor respond to his calls, nor benefit or harm him?"

## Invoking dead righteous people is either *kufr* or madness

"There are two possibilities for those people who turn to the dead for help: either they believe that the dead can hear them from afar, respond to them and save them, or they don't. If they do (as is actually the case) then they are guilty of the greater *shirk,* for which Allah will never forgive them.

"And if they don't, but still turn to them for help, then they are mad, and consequently not accountable for their actions. This means that these grave-worshippers are either polytheists or mad people. I will let you decide which category they belong to.

"The fact of the matter is that these grave-worshippers are not mad, but rather seduced by the devil who made their polytheistic actions seem favourable and alluring to them. If their faith in the powers of those dead righteous people to rescue them from disaster was not greater than their faith in Allah, the Omnipotent and the Exalted One, they would not have turned to the dead imploring them for help with such passion and humility.

"There can be no more serious form of *kufr* and error than this. What have they left for Allah Who created and fashioned them?"

At this point in our discussion, my friend was getting restless; "But ... but ....", he stammered in confusion. He was at a loss for words, so he pretended to be deep in thought.

"There is no 'but' ", I said. "The evidence is crystal clear; you can neither reject it nor refute it. There is nothing to support these polytheistic and idolatrous absurdities except some fallacies, delusions and myths, with which you have demolished your religion and driven yourselves out of Islam."

"Furthermore", I went on, "I believe that after all this explanation and clarification, I don't need to cite any further evidence to convince you that the *shirk,* for which the earlier polytheists were denounced by Allah, was not attributable to their belief that those so-called protectors (such as Yaghuth, Ya'uq, Nasr, Al-Lat, Al-'Uzza and Manat) shared Allah's power to create, give life, cause death, or harm or benefit anybody; nor could it be ascribed to their denial of the existence of Allah or any doubt about His dominion over the universe. None of the earlier polytheists ever expressed such a denial."

## Communism before the advent of Islam

"Of course they did!", he spoke up as if he stumbled upon an overwhelming argument. "The Qur'an quoting some of these polytheists informs us that they denied the existence of Allah:

﴿ وَقَالُوا مَا هِيَ إِلَّا حَيَاتُنَا الدُّنْيَا نَمُوتُ وَنَحْيَا وَمَا يُهْلِكُنَا إِلَّا الدَّهْرُ ... ﴾
الجاثية: ٢٤

*And they say, "What is there but our life in this world? We shall die and we live, and nothing but Time can destroy us ..."*
*[Al-Jathiyah, 45: 24].*

I said to him, "These are not the same polytheists we talked about earlier on. They were rather a group of Arab atheists, in whose footsteps the contemporary communists are following. They neither believed in Allah, nor in anything the polytheists believed would bring them nearer to Allah. In other words, these atheists denied the existence of Allah and, consequently, did not believe in the idols and gods regarded by the polytheists as mediators bringing them closer to Allah.

"The *shirk* committed by the earlier polytheists was attributed to the fact that while they believed in Allah they invoked others for help and sought their intercession with Him on their behalf; this is what Allah was referring to when He said:

﴿ وَمَا يُؤْمِنُ أَكْثَرُهُم بِاللهِ إِلَّا وَهُم مُشْرِكُون ﴾ يوسف: ١٠٦

*And most of them believe not in Allah without associating (others as partners) with Him [Yusuf, 12: 106].*

"If those polytheists did not believe in Allah, they would not have taken these gods as a means of access to Allah, as mentioned in the Qur'an:

﴿ ... وَالَّذِينَ اتَّخَذُوا مِن دُونِهِ أَوْلِيَاءَ مَا نَعْبُدُهُم إِلَّا لِيُقَرِّبُونَا إِلَى الله زُلْفَى ... ﴾ الزمر: ٣

*... Those who take for protectors others than Allah (say): "We only worship them in order that they may bring us nearer to Allah." ... [Az-Zumar, 39: 3].*

"This shows unequivocally that the people mentioned in the verse you cited from the *surah* (chapter of) Al-Jathiyah in support of your argument are not the ones I was talking about, but rather a group of Arab atheists or 'communists', if you like.

28

"It is inconceivable that the earlier polytheists should deny the existence of Allah and then seek to defend and justify their polytheistic stance and their worship of their so-called gods and protectors by saying: 'We only worship them in order that they may bring us nearer to Allah' [Az-Zumar, 39: 3], or 'they are our intercessors with Allah' [Yunus, 10: 4]. It is impossible that such people had no faith in Allah, given that they had only sought the mediation and intercession of their false gods in order to get closer to Him. Moreover, there are many other Qur'anic verses which clearly affirm that they professed a belief in Allah as the One and Only Lord of the universe."

**Nature of the *shirk* committed by the earlier polytheists**

My friend (by now quite exhausted by our long discussion) said, "Now, if those polytheists believed in the existence and oneness of Allah, as you are claiming, what sort of *shirk* was it then, which was condemned in the Qur'an, and for which Allah made it lawful to kill them and confiscate their property, and commanded His messenger to fight them?"

"This is the real question.", I replied. "It is a very crucial issue which people fail to understand. If they considered it carefully, not even a single person claiming to be a Muslim would ever turn to anything or anyone other than Allah for help, invoke them or make vows or offerings to them; because all such forms of devotion are due to Allah alone, and not to anyone else, be they prophets, saints or others."

**Widespread ignorance about the nature of *shirk* committed by the earlier Arab pagans**

"It is people's ignorance in this grave matter and their failure to understand the true nature of the *shirk* committed by the earlier Arab pagans, which led them to indulge in activities that constituted *shirk,* though they did not see them as such. Owing to their ignorance, they failed to realize that their practices were nothing but sheer *kufr* (such as making supplications to the dead, invoking their help, and making vows and offerings to them in the hope that they would intercede with Allah on their behalf and bring them closer to Him). They had no permission whatsoever from Allah to engage in such practices.

### A premonition of *shirk* more than 13 centuries ago

"More than thirteen centuries ago, 'Umar ibn Al-Khattab expressed a premonition of the kind of *shirk* being committed these days. He said, 'The ties of Islam will be broken one after the other.' He was then asked, 'O Commander of the Faithful, how will that happen?'. He replied, 'When there are people born and brought up in Islam, who do not know what *jahiliyah* is.'

"If those people who nowadays call upon the dead, offer sacrifices and make vows to them, and go around their graves in fear, humility and devotion seeking their mediation and intercession with Allah on their behalf – if they knew that all of this was precisely what the Arabs of *jahiliyah* (pre-islamic times) did, and was described as *shirk* and *kufr* by Allah, they would not have engaged or persisted in it; nor would they so bitterly resent any criticism of their actions.

"As for the sort of *shirk* which the earlier polytheists were guilty of, and which you asked me to explain, let me tell you that although these polytheists believed in Allah and His

30

absolute dominion over the entire universe without any partner or helper, they fabricated an innovation which is not based on any evidence; an invention that seemed perfectly sound and appealing to them.

"Without Allah's permission or approval, they had taken some of His creatures (e.g., Al-Lat, Al-'Uzza, Manat, Yaghuth, Ya'uq, and Nasr) as their protectors and intermediaries, to whom they addressed their supplications, offerings and vows. They hoped that these so-called protectors would bring them closer to Allah; that they would intercede for them so that Allah would rid them of their difficulties and fulfil their needs.

"The Qur'an condemned this in these words:

﴿ وَيَعْبُدُونَ مِن دُونِ اللهِ مَا لَا يَضُرُّهُمْ وَلَا يَنفَعُهُمْ وَيَقُولُونَ هَؤُلَاءِ شُفَعَاؤُنَا عِندَ اللهِ قُلْ أَتُنَبِّئُونَ اللهَ بِمَا لَا يَعْلَمُ فِي السَّمَاوَاتِ وَلَا فِي الْأَرْضِ سُبْحَانَهُ وَتَعَالَى عَمَّا يُشْرِكُونَ ﴾ يونس: ١٨

*They serve, besides Allah, what can hurt them not nor profit them, and they say: "These are our intercessors with Allah." Say: "Do you indeed inform Allah of something He knows not, in the heavens or on earth? Glory to Him! And far is He above the partners they ascribe (to Him)!" [Yunus, 10: 18].*

﴿ ... مَالَكُم مِن دُونِهِ مِن وَلِيٍّ وَلَاشَفِيعٍ أَفَلَا تَتَذَكَّرُونَ ﴾ السجدة: ٤

*... You have none, besides Him, to protect or intercede (for you): Will you not then receive admonition? [As-Sajdah, 32: 4].*

31

**Taking others as mediators with Allah is an act of sheer *kufr***

"It is because of this philosophy - the philosophy of seeking mediation and intercession through some dead righteous persons whom they deified - that they called upon them, sought their help, made vows and offerings to them, and went around their graven images and idols, having fondly imagined that through them they would gain access to Allah.

"Such actions and beliefs were condemned by Allah as a form of *shirk* and *kufr*. Consequently, Allah made it legitimate to kill those people and confiscate their property, and prophet Muhammad (peace be upon him) fought against them in the battles of Badr, Uhud, Hunain, Al-Khandaq (Trench), and others. For the same reason, the prophet cut off all ties of blood and kinship with them.

"Allah has described these actions and beliefs of theirs as a form of worshipping someone other than Him, and as associating others with Him. Their actions brought upon them Allah's wrath and made them unworthy of His mercy, because they took this path of innovation, of seeking intermediaries and intercessors with Allah, reposing their hopes and trust in them, and turning to them as their means of access to Allah, without any warrant or authority from Him."

﴿ ... مَن ذَا الَّذِي يَشْفَعُ عِندَهُ إِلَّا بِإِذْنِهِ ... ﴾ البقرة: ٢٥٥

*... Who is there that can intercede in His presence except as He permits ... [Al-Baqarah, 2: 255].*

My friend commented, "This is just a general statement without any conclusive argument to support it. Have you got any detailed evidence for what you are saying?"

32

"The evidence can also be found in the Qur'an", I replied. "Allah says:

﴿ يَاأَيُّهَا النَّاسُ ضُرِبَ مَثَلٌ فَاسْتَمِعُوا لَهُ إِنَّ الَّذِينَ تَدْعُونَ مِن دُونِ اللهِ لَن يَخْلُقُوا ذُبَابًا وَلَوِ اجْتَمَعُوا لَهُ وَإِن يَسْلُبْهُمُ الذُّبَابُ شَيْئًا لاَيَسْتَنقِذُوهُ مِنهُ ضَعُفَ الطَّالِبُ وَالمَطْلُوبُ ﴾ الحج: ٧٣

*O men! Here is a parable set forth! Listen to it! Those on*
*whom, besides Allah, you call, cannot create (even) a fly,*
*if they all met together for the purpose! And if the fly*
*should snatch away anything from them, they would have*
*no power to release it from the fly. Feeble are those who*
*petition and those on whom they petition! [Al-Hajj, 22: 73].*

"The Qur'an has likewise condemned these people in *surah*
Yunus (verse 18) for making supplication to anyone other
than Allah, taking them as mediators and intercessors with
Him. The Qur'an described this as associating others with
Allah in His divinity and worshipping them instead of Him:

﴿ وَيَعْبُدُونَ مِن دُونِ اللهِ مَا لا يَضُرُّهُم وَ لا يَنفَعُهُم وَيَقُولُونَ هَؤُلاءِ شُفَعَاؤُنَا عِندَ اللهِ ... ﴾ يونس: ١٨

*They serve, besides Allah, things that hurt them not nor profit*
*them, and they say: "They are our intercessors with Allah ...*
*[Yunus, 10: 18]*

"The Qur'an refuted this false assertion of theirs concerning
intercession and mediation by others with Allah, saying:

﴿ ... قُل أَتُنَبِّئُونَ اللهَ بِمَا لا يَعْلَمُ فِي السَّمَاوَاتِ وَلا فِي الأَرضِ سُبْحَانَهُ وَتَعَالَى عَمَّا يُشْرِكُونَ ﴾ يونس: ١٨

33

*... Say: "Do you indeed inform Allah of something He knows not, in the heavens or on earth? Glory to Him! And far is he above the partners they ascribe (to Him)!" [Yunus, 10: 18]*

"Allah does not need intercession or mediation by anyone in this world, because nothing about His creatures is hidden from Him so that they may require any intercessor or mediator to inform Him of something He is not aware of! Glory be to Him! He is far above their false assertions!

"Condemning the polytheists for seeking the intercession of some devout people whom they held in such high esteem, Allah told them that those pious people were also His servants like them without any power to bring any benefit or avert any harm from themselves, let alone rid them of any affliction or protect them from any harm. In fact, despite their closeness to Allah, those devout people would seek Allah's favour through fearing Him and aspiring after His mercy. Allah says:

﴿ قُل ادْعُوا الذِّينَ زَعَمتم مِن دُونِهِ فَلا يَمْلِكُونَ كَشْفَ الضُّرِّ عَنكُم وَلا تَحويلاً ∗ أُولَئِكَ الذِّينَ يَدْعُونَ يَبْتَغُونَ إِلَى رَبِّهِمُ الوَسِيلَةَ أَيُّهُم أَقْرَبُ وَيَرْجُونَ رَحْمَتَهُ وَيَخَافُونَ عَذَابَهُ إِنَّ عَذَابَ رَبِّكَ كَانَ مَحذُوراً ﴾

الإسراء ٥٦ – ٥٧

*Say: "Call on those - besides Him - whom you fancy: they have neither the power to remove your troubles from you nor to change them." Those whom they[5] call upon do seek (for themselves) means of access to their Lord - even those who*

---

5 - *In another reading 'you'.*

*are nearest: they hope for His mercy and fear His wrath:
for the wrath of your Lord is something to take heed of.
[Al-Isra', 17: 56-57].*

"Allah has described making supplications to any of His creatures as *shirk* (i.e. associating them with Allah):

﴿ ... وَالَّذِينَ تَدْعُونَ مِن دُونِهِ مَا يَمْلِكُونَ مِن قِطْمِيرٍ ٭ إِن تَدْعُوهُمْ
لَا يَسْمَعُوا دُعَاءَكُمْ وَلَو سَمِعُوا مَا استَجَابُوا لَكُم وَيَومَ القِيَامَةِ
يَكْفُرُونَ بِشِرْكِكُم وَلَا يُنَبِّئُكَ مِثْلُ خَبِيرٍ ﴾ فاطر: ١٣ – ١٤

*... And those whom you invoke besides Him own not a straw. If
you invoke them, they will not listen to your call, and if they were
to listen, they cannot answer your (prayer). On the Day of
Judgment they will reject your 'partnership'. And none,
(O man!) can inform you like Him Who is All-Aware.
[Fatir, 35: 13-14].*

﴿ لَهُ دَعْوَةُ الحَقِّ وَالذِينَ يَدْعُونَ مِن دُونِهِ لَا يَسْتَجِيبُونَ لَهُم بِشَيءٍ
إِلَّا كَبَاسِطِ كَفَّيْهِ إِلَى المَاءِ لِيَبْلُغَ فَاهُ وَمَا هُوَ بِبَالِغِهِ وَمَا دُعَاءُ الكَافِرِينَ
إِلَّا فِي ضَلَالٍ ﴾ الرعد: ١٤

*To Him is due the true prayer; any others that they call upon
besides Him hear them no more than if they were to stretch forth
their hands for water to reach their mouths, but it reaches them
not: for the prayer of those without faith is nothing but vain
prayer. [Ar-Ra'd, 13: 14].*

﴿ ... وَالذِينَ اتَّخَذُوا مِن دُونِهِ أَولِيَاءَ مَا نَعْبُدُهُم إِلَّا لِيُقَرِّبُونَا إِلَى
اللهِ زُلْفَى إِنَّ اللهَ يَحْكُمُ بَيْنَهُم فِي مَا هُم فِيهِ يَخْتَلِفُونَ إِنَّ اللهَ
لَا يَهْدِي مَن هُوَ كَاذِبٌ كَفَّارٌ ﴾ الزمر: ٣

35

*... But those who take for protectors others than Allah (say):
"We only serve them in order that they may bring us nearer to
Allah." Truly Allah will judge between them in that wherein they
differ. But Allah guides not such as are false and ungrateful.*
*[Az-Zumar, 39: 3].*

"These are some, and by no means all, of the arguments that
support the truth of what I have told you about the earlier
polytheists and the nature of their *shirk*. It is the same kind of
*shirk* a lot of people commit out of ignorance of its nature."

### Demolishing the biggest fallacy the grave-worshippers have been clinging to

My friend said, "The verses you have quoted were revealed
about the Arab pagans of *jahiliyah* (pre-Islamic time) and they
apply to them only. They have no bearing on those who
nowadays invoke dead pious people for help, nor do they
apply to them."

"This is a false argument and a manifest distortion", I
remarked. "It is true that these verses were revealed at the time
of the Arab pagans, but so was the whole Qur'an; it is an
eternal Book revealed by Allah for mankind of all times and
climes, with commands and prohibitions for them to abide by
till the Day of Judgement.

"The decisive consideration in interpreting the Qur'an is the
general signification of its words rather than the special occasion
of their revelation. The established principle in this regard, on
which there is a general consensus among Muslims, is that the
commands depend on their causes; whenever the cause is found,
the relevant command must automatically take effect.

"The reason why the earlier polytheists were described as guilty of *shirk* was that they called upon others besides Allah, who were humans like themselves, and relied on them to intercede with Allah on their behalf. This is precisely what the grave-worshippers of today are doing: calling upon dead people and invoking them as mediators who provide access to Allah. For this reason, both groups are judged to be equally guilty of committing *shirk* (without any distinction). There is no difference between them as far as intentions and actions are concerned; they both turned to someone other than Allah and addressed their supplications, offerings and vows to them in the hope that they would intercede with Allah on their behalf."

He said, "The analogy on the basis of which you have placed the two groups on a par with each other as far as *shirk* is concerned ignores some important differences, and is, therefore, unacceptable."

"I have gone to great lengths to explain to you that the *kufr* attributed to the earlier polytheists consisted in the fact that they sought mediators and intercessors and aspired to win their favour by addressing their supplications, offerings and vows to them.", I replied. "I have also explained that the grave-worshippers we see nowadays are following exactly the same path. Can you now explain to me the differences between the two groups? Can you explain to me why the actions of those earlier pagans are to be regarded as pure *kufr* and *shirk*, punishable by eternal fire, while those of grave-worshippers should be deemed as a means of seeking allegedly permissible intercession even though there is hardly any difference between the two groups as far as their intentions and actions are concerned?"

He replied, "There are several differences between them: firstly, the earlier polytheists worshipped others besides Allah as they themselves clearly confessed:

$$\{ ... \ \text{مَا نَعْبُدُهُم إِلَّا لِيُقَرِّبُونَا إِلَى اللهِ زُلْفَى} \ ... \} \ \text{الزمر: ٣}$$

*"... We worship them not but that they should bring us closer to Allah. ..." [Az-Zumar, 39: 3]*

"But those who seek means of access to Allah through dead righteous people repudiate worshipping anyone other than Allah. They clearly assert that by turning to dead devout people and invoking their help, they do not mean to worship them; they merely seek their blessings and their intercession with Allah. This clearly distinguishes them from the polytheists."

**Changing words does not alter facts**

I said to him, "As I told you earlier, it is actions and intentions that form the basis of any judgment. The words a person uses to defend his actions and ward off any adverse judgment are immaterial so long as his actions warrant this judgment against him. If a person, for instance, persistently prostrates to idols, and at the same time denounces worshipping any one other than Allah, and declares that he has never worshipped, and will never worship, anyone other than Allah, would this protestation of his (which is contradicted by his actions) ward off a verdict of *kufr* and *shirk* against him?"

My friend replied, "No, such a person is indeed a *kafir* and a *mushrik*." [6]

---

6 - A *'kafir'* is a disbeliever, and a *'mushrik'* is a person who associates any partner with Allah.

"This is perfectly applicable to the grave-worshippers of today.", I said. "By their actions they stand convicted of *shirk* and *kufr,* but despite this manifest guilt they continue to deny it.

"The only difference between them and the earlier polytheists is that while the latter were more candid in their confession of worshipping others besides Allah, the former resort to deception, distortion, and casuistry. They worship others besides Allah, but refuse to call a spade a spade and insist on labelling it as something else."

Trying to confuse me, he said, "I have already told you, and will keep repeating that the earlier polytheists worshipped others besides Allah, and were rightly described as guilty of *shirk* and *kufr.* But the actions of those who turn to dead righteous people for help and intercession with Allah are in a different category, and cannot be regarded as *kufr* or *shirk.*"

I said to him, "I am frustrated by your repeated attempts to avoid admitting the plain truth, which could not conceivably be denied by a sensible person like yourself.

"I have made it abundantly clear to you that the earlier polytheists had faith in Allah and believed in His Oneness (as the only Lord, Creator and Sustainer of the worlds). I have also explained to you in detail the nature of the *shirk* they committed, and the reasons why they were judged to be guilty of it.

"I have clarified that our judgement that grave-worshippers are guilty of *shirk* is based on a comparison between their actions and those of the earlier polytheists, on whom the

Qur'an gave its verdict more than thirteen hundred years ago. After close scrutiny and sound comparison, we concluded that the actions of present-day grave-worshippers, namely supplicating dead righteous people, invoking their help, making offerings and vows to them, and looking to them with hope and fear, are nothing but a form of worshipping someone other than Allah, the Exalted One.

"It was precisely this kind of behaviour on the part of the earlier polytheists with regard to their 'saints' and others they turned to, that was described by Allah as worshipping others besides Him.

"But you still insist on making a distinction between the two groups even though they both, through their common actions and intentions, worship something or someone other than Allah.

"And if that is still your opinion could you please explain to me in detail the nature of worship which the polytheists addressed to others besides Allah, and for which they were deemed to have committed *shirk* and *kufr.*"

**Making supplications, offerings and vows to anyone other than Allah is the major form of *shirk***

"I'd like you to explain this issue in order for us to understand if there is any difference between the two groups. This will also help us check the validity of your standpoint, whereby you regard the actions of the earlier polytheists as 'worship' of someone other than Allah, but refuse to regard those of grave-worshippers as such."

At this point he was apparently perplexed and embarrassed. My question must have descended on him like a stinging whip.

He was now facing a dilemma, but was not ready to capitulate. Yet in his confusion he admitted to a fact that he had been denying all along. He said, "The truth which must be admitted is that the earlier polytheists did no more than seek to gain their idols' favour through supplications, sacrifices, vows and other rituals addressed to them, even though they believed that those idols had no power to create, to give sustenance, to give life or cause death, nor to avert any harm or bestow any good on anyone."

"Their purpose in what they did", he continued, "was to please these idols so that they would bring them closer to Allah and intercede with Him on their behalf to bless them with His mercy, care, and protection.

"This was the true nature of their worship of others besides Allah, because of which Allah described them as polytheists and judged them to be guilty of *kufr*. I must confess that before this discussion I did not know the real nature of the *shirk* attributed to the earlier polytheists."

"Great!", I exclaimed. "This means that we have at last agreed on one of the most important points under discussion, namely the nature of worship addressed by the earlier polytheists to their gods. You must also agree that making supplications, vows and offerings to them, the ritual of going around them and other similar acts of devotion performed in subservience and humility are all tantamount to worshipping them."

**There is no difference between the present-day grave-worshippers and the polytheists of old**

"Now that you have correctly answered my first question", I

41

went on, "I'd like you to answer another question just as candidly. Isn't it true that the grave-worshippers of today turn to dead people for help, make supplications, offerings and vows to them, and go round their graves, in extreme humility and devotion, in the hope that they would be pleased with them and would intercede on their behalf with Allah?"

"Yes, it is.", he answered; "This is precisely what they do; there is no denying it."

I said to him, "We agree then that the two groups are identical in this regard: the grave-worshippers turn to dead righteous people with supplications, sacrifices, going round their graves, in humility and devotion, just as the early polytheists did with idols they worshipped besides Allah. In both cases, worship is devoted to someone other than Allah, which is precisely what is called *shirk* and is explicitly forbidden by Allah.

"What, then, keeps you from admitting that by their actions grave-worshippers are guilty of the sin of *shirk* (associating others with Allah) given that their intentions and actions are no different from those of the early polytheists?"

### Is there any real difference between invoking idols and statues and invoking dead righteous people?

He replied, "What prevents me from accepting it is that the early polytheists turned to idols and statues which were made by their own hands, and on which no standing or status was conferred by Allah, whereas the people you call 'grave-worshippers' turn to dead devout people who occupy a high position and status in Allah's sight. Allah Himself said:

42

﴾ أَلَا إِنَّ أَوْلِيَاءَ اللهِ لَا خَوْفٌ عَلَيْهِم وَلَا هُم يَحْزَنُونَ ﴿ يونس: ٦٢

*Behold! surely on the friends of Allah there is no fear, nor shall they grieve. [Yunus, 10: 62].*

"There is a great difference between the stones and idols the polytheists worshipped as their gods, and the dead righteous men who are not regarded as gods by those who invoke them for help."

I said to him, "It seems I was too optimistic earlier on when I thought you put your feet firmly on the right track and were beginning to see the truth at last. But I am sorry to see you go back to the same vicious circle of evasions and false arguments.

"Your differentiation between the two groups is extremely foolish and misconceived. Your argument is too flimsy to merit serious consideration, let alone gain acceptance.

"It is a well-established principle among Muslims that worshipping someone other than Allah, in any shape or form, is in fact a negation of one's faith in Allah *(kufr)* and a form of *shirk* that drives one out of the faith of Islam. In this regard it makes no difference who those called upon are: the prophets of Allah, His messengers, His angels, righteous people, saints or stones, idols or the accursed devil. The fact which is not disputed by any Muslim is that worshipping anyone other than Allah constitutes *kufr* and *shirk*.

"You yourself have admitted in the course of this discussion that supplicating, making vows and offerings and performing other rituals, such as going round graves, are all forms of worship.

43

"You regard the actions of the polytheists as worship of their idols and statues and a clear rejection of Allah, yet you insist that similar actions performed by the grave-worshippers and aimed at the dead in their tombs do not constitute worshipping them or associating them with Allah. This is quite an arbitrary stance and a deviation from the truth. It is an unfortunate attempt to deny the obvious, just like denying the existence of the sun or the moon!

"The distinction you have made between the two groups, is neither supported by any evidence from the Qur'an or *hadith,* nor can it be substantiated by any rational argument. It is in fact an expression of arrogance and stubbornness which, in spite of our long discussion, still keep a strong hold on you.", I said with some irritation.

He replied, "I'm neither arrogant nor stubborn. Just like you, I have the right to express my opinions and beliefs, and this is what I still believe in. We agreed right from the start of this discussion to be frank with each other and to lay our feelings and emotions aside. So please do not get angry and let me express all my views freely. If you do not agree with any of them, you have the right to refute it with whatever evidence or arguments you have, but let it be a rational, dispassionate dialogue, free from any harsh words or emotional reaction. Otherwise our discussion would be futile."

"I do agree with you that getting annoyed or using harsh words in a discussion would defeat its purpose.", I conceded. "I will do my best, though, to bring you out of what I sincerely believe is error."

## The *shirk* of the earlier polytheists was attributed to nothing but worshipping dead righteous people

"You still insist on drawing an unjustifiable distinction between the two groups as far as *shirk* is concerned. Your argument, or rather fallacy, for this distinction is that the earlier polytheists worshipped idols made of stone in the hope that they would bring them closer to Allah, and that present-day grave-worshippers only turn to righteous people. I am prepared to demolish this flimsy argument and dispel any doubt still lingering in your mind by proving to you that the earlier polytheists were identical to the grave-worshippers we see today; they, too, addressed their offerings, vows, supplications and other rituals to mortals, whom they regarded as pious and righteous. Indeed, they worshipped none but those pious people.

"They did not worship the statues and idols in their own right, but rather the people those idols symbolized and were named after (such as Yaghuth, Ya'uq, Wadd, Suwa', Al-Lat and Al-'Uzza).

"Now, the proof that the earlier polytheists, like present-day grave-worshippers, worshipped and deified righteous people besides Allah is in the Qur'an, but you fail to see it. Addressing all polytheists, Allah *subhanahu wa ta'ala* said:

﴿ إِنَّ الذِينَ تَدْعُونَ مِن دُونِ اللهِ عِبَادٌ أَمْثَالُكُم فَادْعُوهُم فَلْيَسْتَجِيبُوا لَكُم إِن كُنتُم صَادِقِينَ ﴾ الأعراف: ١٩٤

*Verily those whom you call upon beside Allah are servants like you: Call upon them, then, and let them answer to your prayer, if you are indeed truthful!. [Al-A'raf, 7: 194]*

45

﴿ مَثَلُ الذِينَ اتَّخَذُوا مِن دُونِ اللهِ أولِيَاءَ كَمَثَلِ العَنكَبُوتِ اتَّخَذَتْ بَيتاً وَإِنَّ أوْهَنَ البُيُوتِ لَبَيتُ العَنكَبُوتِ لَوْ كَانُوا يَعْلَمُونَ ﴾ العنكبوت: ٤١

*The parable of those who take protectors other than Allah is that of the Spider who builds (to itself) a house; but truly the flimsiest of houses is the Spider's house; if they but knew.*
*[Al-'Ankabut, 29: 41]*

"Laying down a general rule of worship for all, which is valid in all times and places, Allah Almighty said:

﴿ ألا للهِ الدِّينُ الخَالِصُ والذِينَ اتَّخَذُوا مِن دُونِهِ أوْلِيَاءَ مَانَعْبُدُهُم إلا لِيُقَرِّبُونَا إلَى اللهِ زُلْفَى ... ﴾ الزمر: ٣

*Now surely all sincere devotion is due to Allah. But those who take for protectors others than Allah (say): "We only serve them in order that they may bring us nearer to Allah. ..."*
*[Az-Zumar, 39: 3]*

﴿ قُل مَن رَبُّ السَّمَاوَاتِ والأرض قُل اللهُ قُل أفَاتَّخَذْتُم مِن دُونِهِ أوْلِيَاءَ لاَيَمْلِكُونَ لأنفُسِهِم نَفْعاً وَلاضَراً ... ﴾ الرعد: ١٦

*Say: Do you then take (for worship) protectors other than Him, such as have no power either for good or for harm to themselves? [Ar-Ra'd, 13: 16]*

﴿ أفَحَسِبَ الذِينَ كَفَرُوا أن يَتَّخِذُوا عِبَادِي مِن دُونِي أوْلِيَاءَ .... ﴾ الكهف: ١٠٢

*Do the unbelievers think that they can take My servants as protectors besides Me? ... [Al-Kahf, 18: 102]*

﴿ أم اتَّخَذُوا مِن دُونِهِ أُولِيَاءَ فَاللهُ هُوَ الْوَلِيُّ ..... ﴾ الشورى: ٩

*What! Have they taken (for worship) protectors besides Him?*
*But it is Allah - He is the Protector. ... [Ash-Shura, 42: 9]*

﴿ قُل أغَيْرَ اللهِ أتَّخِذُ وَلِياً فَاطِرِ السَّمَاوَاتِ والأرضِ ..... ﴾ الأنعام: ١٤

*Say: "Shall I take for my protector any other than Allah,*
*the Maker of the heavens and the earth?" .. [Al-An'am, 6: 14]*

These noble verses prove beyond doubt that, like present-day
grave-worshippers, earlier polytheists turned to *auliya'*, i.e.
saints and righteous people, for help and protection, and that
they worshipped them as gods, made supplications, offerings
and vows to them, feared them, and implored them to
intercede on their behalf and seek to bring them closer to
Allah."

**The earlier polytheists did not worship the idols for their own
sake**

"The verses I have just quoted from the Qur'an also prove
that the statues, graven images and other idols (such as Al-
Lat, Al-'Uzza, Manah, Yaghuth, Ya'uq and Nasr) actually
stood for, and consequently were named after, some godly
people.

"The earlier polytheists did not worship these idols as such,
but rather the people symbolized by them; they held them in
high esteem and believed them to be righteous and godly
protectors, just as grave-worshippers do today.

"This shows clearly that the two parties, the grave-worshippers and the earlier polytheists, are no different as far as worshipping righteous people is concerned. The only difference between them is that the earlier polytheists were devoted to the worship of statues and idols named after certain pious people they regarded as their protectors, whereas the grave-worshippers of our time addressed their devotions to graves, coffins, shrines and mausoleums bearing the names of dead righteous people. In both cases, the devotion is ultimately intended not for the idols or graves but rather for the people they are named after.

"Ask any of those grave-worshippers who have just returned from a visit to a shrine, for example Al-Badawi's, 'where have you been?''; he or she would reply, 'to sidi[7] Al-Badawi', even though they have never met him or even seen him. They have only been to the grave or shrine bearing his name. The same would apply to earlier polytheists, who did not actually turn to their so-called protectors (Al-Lat, Yaghuth, Ya'uq, etc.), but rather to the statues and idols named after them."

### Idols were merely the names of righteous men

At this point, my interlocutor asked, "Where is your proof that the earlier polytheists did not worship the idols and statues made of stone, gold or copper in their own right, but rather worshipped some *auliya'* or righteous people after whom those images and objects were named?"

"You should have been able by now to extract the conclusive proof from the noble verses I quoted earlier from the Qur'an",

---

7 - *'Saiyidi', colloquially pronounced 'sidi', is an honorific title literally meaning 'my lord' or 'my master'.*

I replied[8]; "They unequivocally prove that the earlier polytheists worshipped nothing but righteous and pious people (supposed to have lived and died long before).

"But to make things yet clearer, I will cite further evidence in support of my assertion. This, I hope, should dispel any lingering doubt and demolish any spurious counter-argument you may still be holding on to."

## Yaghuth, Ya'uq and Nasr were righteous people from the nation of prophet Noah (peace be upon him)

(1) Al-Bukhari reported ibn 'Abbas (may Allah be pleased with him), to have said: "... The idols worshipped by the nation of prophet Noah ended up being worshipped by the Arab tribes: Wadd was adopted by the tribe of Kalb (in the region of Daumat Al-Jandal); Suwa' was worshipped by Hudhail, and Yaghuth by Murad and then Banu Ghutaif (in the region of Al-Hauf or Al-Jurf) near Saba'.

'The idols Ya'uq and Nasr were worshipped by Hamadan, Himyar and the clan of Dhal-Kala', respectively. All these idols had been named after righteous men from the nation of prophet Noah (peace be upon him), Whenever any of these men died, his people, inspired by the devil, would erect a monument to him where he used sit (among his followers), and name it after him. Monuments were thus built but not worshipped; when generations succeeded one another and

---

8 - *It has been already explained that the worship of any entity other than Allah, for which the earlier polytheists were condemned in the Qur'an, encompassed invoking, fearing or beseeching idols named after dead righteous people, or making sacrifices or vows to them.*

knowledge was gradually obliterated and corrupted, they began to be worshipped.'

(2) Similarly, in his book entitled *Al-Asnam* (the idols), Al-Kalbi said: "Then came the third generation and thought, 'Our ancestors had only exalted those (righteous men) because they were seeking their intercession with Allah'; so they worshipped them." [P. 52]

(3) Referring to Wadd, Suwa', Yaghuth, Ya'uq and Nasr, Muhammad ibn Ka'b said: "These are the names of devout people who lived in the period between the time of Adam and Noah (peace be upon them). When they died they left behind people who followed their example and copied them in worship. Satan then whispered to them, 'If you made images of those righteous men, you would be more keen on worship'; so they did. Then came another generation, to whom Satan whispered, 'Those who lived before you used to worship them'; so they, too, worshipped them."

### When did idol worship start?

"That is how idol worship started. The images were named after those righteous Muslims because they were made to look like them.

Muhammad ibn Qais was reported by ibn Jarir to have said: "These were righteous people who lived in the time intervening between Adam and Noah (peace be upon them). There came after them people who followed their example and thought, 'If we made images of those righteous ancestors, they would remind us of them, and this should make us more zealous in worshipping"; consequently, they made effigies of them."

50

Similar accounts were ascribed to 'Ikrimah, Ad-Dahhak, Qatadah and ibn Ishaq.

### Al-Lat was a man who used to make a meal of barley and wheat and offer it to pilgrims

(4) As for Al-Lat, ibn 'Abbas is reported by al-Bukhari to have said: "Al-Lat was a man who used to mix *saweeq*.[9] " Likewise, in his book entitled *Al-Asnam* (the idols) [p.16], ibn Al-Kalbi writes: "Al-Lat was a square rock in At-Ta'if, which was not as old as Manat. By that rock, a jew used to mix *saweeq.*"

(5) Ash-Shahristani, author of *Al-Milal wan-Nihal* (Religions and Sects), says: "Idols, whenever and wherever they are erected, can only be conceived as representations of an absent deity who is thought to be alive; idols are made in his form and are considered to be representing him. For we know with certainty that no sane person would carve an image with his own hands and then believe it to be a god. But when people regularly turned to idols and habitually relied upon them to fulfil their needs without any proof, permission or authority from Allah Almighty, their actions were tantamount to worshipping and deifying them. Hence their claim:

$$ \text{٣ :الزمر} \quad \text{﴾} ...... \text{زُلْفَى} \text{ اللهِ} \text{ إِلَى} \text{ لِيُقَرِّبُونَا} \text{ إلا} \text{ مَانَعْبُدُهُم} ... \text{﴿} $$

*... We only worship them in order that they bring us nearer to Allah ... [Az-Zumar, 39: 3]*

---

9 - *A kind of mush or porridge made of wheat or barley (also with sugar and dates). The word Al-Lat is an active participle denoting the agent of the verb 'yaluttu', which means 'to knead, roll or moisten (esp. saweeq) by mixing with water (or fat)'.*

"Having heard all of this", I asked my friend, "do you still have any lingering doubt about the fact that idols were made for, and named after, certain persons, who were considered righteous and were loved by their people? Or that these statues were not themselves worshipped but rather the persons for whom they were made and after whom they were named?"

## A major problem resolved

Having apparently recognized the soundness of my argument, he said, "There are still considerable problematic areas which need to be resolved. We read in the Qur'an, for instance,

﴿ وَإِذْ قَالَ إِبْرَاهِيمُ رَبِّ اجْعَلْ هَذَا الْبَلَدَ ءَامِناً وَاجْنُبْنِي وَبَنِيَّ أن نَعْبُدَ الْأَصْنَامَ ﴾ إبراهيم: ٣٥

*Remember Abraham said: "O my Lord! make this city one of peace and security: and preserve me and my sons from worshipping idols. [Ibrahim, 14: 35].*

I asked him to explain what seems to be problematic and promised to resolve it for him.

He said, "It would seem from the Qur'anic verses and traditions you quoted earlier on that you wanted to establish that the early polytheists in reality worshipped their saints and pious persons, in order to show by analogy that the grave-worshippers, as you call them, likewise worship dead righteous people.

But the verses quoted about the polytheists state that they worshipped the idols as such; if they did not, but rather worshipped the devout persons after whom those idols were

52

named, Allah would have surely told us so. In such a case, the Qur'an would have only reprimanded the polytheists for worshipping saintly people, given that they only worshipped those saints and that they did not rely on their idols to intercede with Allah on their behalf.

"In most cases, the Qur'an warns these polytheists against, and condemn them for, worshipping idols, stones, and images:

﴿ ... فَاجْتَنِبُوا الرِّجْسَ مِنَ الأَوْثَانِ وَاجْتَنِبُوا قَوْلَ الزُّورِ ﴾ الحج: ٣٠

*And shun the abomination of idols, and shun the word that is false. [Al-Hajj, 22: 30).*

﴿ إِنَّمَا تَعْبُدُونَ مِنْ دُونِ اللهِ أَوْثَاناً وَتَخْلُقُونَ إِفْكاً ... ﴾ العنكبوت: ١٧

*You do worship idols besides Allah, and you invent falsehood. [Al-'Ankabut, 29: 17].*

﴿ وَقَالَ إِنَّمَا اتَّخَذْتُم مِّن دُونِ اللهِ أَوْثَاناً مَوَدَّةَ بَيْنِكُم فِي الحياةِ الدُّنْيَا ...﴾ العنكبوت: ٢٥

*And he said, 'You have taken (for worship) idols besides Allah, out of mutual love and regard between yourselves in this life. [Al-'Ankabut, 29: 25].*

﴿ ... فَأَتَوْا عَلَى قَوْمٍ يَعْكُفُونَ عَلَى أَصْنَامٍ لَهُم ... ﴾ الأعراف: ١٣٨

*They came upon a people devoted entirely to some idols. [Al-A'raf, 7: 138].*

﴿ وَإِذْ قَالَ إِبْرَاهِيمُ لِأَبِيهِ ءَازَرَ أَتَتَّخِذُ أَصْنَاماً ءَالِهَةً ... ﴾ الأنعام: ٧٤

53

*Lo! Abraham said to his father Azar: Do you take idols for gods?*
*[Al-An'am, 6: 74].*

﴿ قَالُوا نَعْبُدُ أَصْنَاماً فَنَظَلُّ لَهَا عَاكِفِين ﴾ الشعراء: ٧١

*They said, "We worship idols, and we remain constantly in*
*attendance on them." [Ash-Shu'ara', 26: 71].*

﴿ وَتَاللهِ لَأَكِيدَنَّ أَصْنَامَكُم بَعْدَ أَن تُوَلُّوا مُدْبِرِينَ ﴾ الأنبياء: ٥٧

*"And by Allah, I have a plan for your idols - after you go away*
*and turn your backs. [Al-Anbiya', 21: 57].*

﴿ وَلَقَدْ ءَاتَيْنَا إِبْرَاهِيمَ رُشْدَهُ مِن قَبْلُ وَكُنَّا بِهِ عَالِمِينَ * إِذْ قَالَ لِأَبِيهِ وَقَوْمِهِ مَاهَذِهِ
التَّمَاثِيلُ الَّتِي أَنتُم لَهَا عَاكِفُون ﴾ الأنبياء: ٥١ – ٥٢

*We bestowed aforetime on Abraham his rectitude of conduct,*
*and well were we acquainted with him. Behold! he said to his*
*father and his people, 'What are these images to which you are*
*(so assiduously) devoted?' [Al Anbiya', 21: 51-52].*

These verses highlight the fact that the earlier polytheists
worshipped idols and images in their own right. Therefore, idol
worship was explicitly prohibited, and so was worship of
saintly people."

### Idol worship was in fact worship of dead righteous people

"True, the prohibition of worshipping idols or dead righteous
people is well-established", I affirmed. "This explicitly
incriminates grave-worshippers as guilty of worshipping
others besides Allah, because they do indeed worship the
dead. If the Qur'an had forbidden only the worship of others

besides Allah, mentioning only the idols but not the *auliya'*, (righteous people) we would still regard those people who turn to the graves as worshippers of saintly persons because they devote to them the same kind of worship devoted by the earlier polytheists to their idols (supplications, offerings, vows, invoking them in fear and hope); that is obviously assuming that the earlier polytheists worshipped idols, images and statues made of stone, copper, gold and other similar inanimate objects.

"But it is a proven fact that these polytheists did worship saints and other righteous persons in their own right. They did not worship the idols and images as such but rather their real gods: the devout persons after whom these idols, statues, and images were named, as I have already explained with conclusive evidence.

"That is why Allah sometimes described them as 'worshippers of idols' and sometimes as ' worshippers of *auliya'* '. They worshipped the idols by turning to them, going around them, staying close to them, and offering sacrifices in their names.

"They were also worshippers of *auliya'* as they made supplications to those saintly people represented by the idols, entreated them to fulfil their needs, and relied upon them to intercede with Allah for them without any permission from Him.

"Likewise, the grave-worshippers we see today kiss the coverings of the tombs, go around them, embellish them with domes, and offer sacrifices to them. They are, in the first place, quite manifestly worshippers of graves and, by implication, worshippers of dead righteous people.

"Circling around the tombs, they invoke the dead and seek their help, support, and protection, which shows that they openly worship dead devout people and implicitly worship graves.

"So you would be right to call them 'grave-worshippers', given what they do with regard to the graves; and if you described them as worshippers of dead saintly people, you would still be right, given that they fear them, pin their hopes on them and devote their supplications, vows, and offerings to them, which is all tantamount to worshipping them.

"In either case, they are committing major *shirk*. You would also be right to describe them as slaves of their whims and delusions. A grave-worshipper is deluded by caprice into this kind of worship. The images he conjures up and the actions he performs in tombs are the result of his whims and desires.

"Let me quote 'Abdur Rahman Al-Wakil, who in his book entitled *Da'watul Haq* [page 62], writes:

**The reason why the Qur'an uses both relative pronouns *'man'* (who) and *'ma'* (what) to denote the polytheists' gods**

"This explains why the qur'an uses both relative pronouns *'man'* (who) and *'ma'* (what), which denote rational and non-rational beings respectively, in the same narration or even interchangeably in the same context.

"Whenever it is used, the pronoun *'ma'* denotes the idols and statues named after saintly people. The difference in denotation is determined from a subjective point of view. Both pronouns denote those 'others' worshipped besides

Allah, with 'man' referring to the persons themselves who were worshipped and 'ma' to the statues or idols bearing their names. The Qur'an says,

﴿ وَمَن أَضَلُّ مِمَّن يَدْعُوا مِن دُونِ اللهِ مَن لا يَسْتَجِيبُ لَهُ إِلَى يَوْمِ القِيَامَةِ وَهُم عَن دُعَائِهِم غَافِلُونَ ﴾ الأحقاف: ٥

*And who is more astray than one who invokes, beside Allah, those who will not answer him to the Day of Judgement? ...*
*[Al-Ahqaf, 46: 5]*

In the previous verse in the same *surah* the Qur'an says:

﴿ قُلْ أَرَأَيْتُم مَا تَدْعُونَ مِن دُونِ اللهِ أَرُونِي مَاذَا خَلَقُوا مِن الأَرضِ ... ﴾
الأحقاف: ٤

*Say: "Do you see what it is you invoke beside Allah? Show me what it is they have created on earth? ... [Al-Ahqaf, 46: 4]*

"So both pronouns, *'ma'* (what) and *'man'* (who), have the same denotation.

"You should not be deceived or swayed by those grave-worshippers' false claim that the *shirk* of the earlier polytheists in *jahiliyah* (pre-islamic time) was attributable to invoking idols. That is why, they say, that the Qur'an when referring to them uses the pronoun *'ma'*, which denotes non-rational beings, 'but we only invoke saintly people.'

"From this explanation it is clear that the Qur'an uses the pronouns *'man'* and *'ma'* interchangeably in the same context:

﴿ وَاتْلُ عَلَيْهِم نَبَأَ إِبْرَاهِيمَ ۞ إِذْ قَالَ لِأَبِيهِ وَقَوْمِهِ مَا تَعْبُدُونَ ۞ قَالُوا نَعْبُدُ أَصْنَامًا فَنَظَلُّ لَهَا عَاكِفِينَ ۞ قَالَ هَلْ يَسْمَعُونَكُمْ إِذْ تَدْعُونَ ۞ أَوْ يَنفَعُونَكُمْ أَوْ يَضُرُّونَ ۞ قَالُوا بَلْ وَجَدْنَا ءَابَاءَنَا كَذَلِكَ يَفْعَلُونَ ۞ قَالَ أَفَرَأَيْتُم مَّاكُنتُمْ تَعْبُدُونَ ۞ أَنتُمْ وَءَابَاؤُكُمُ الْأَقْدَمُونَ ۞ فَإِنَّهُمْ عَدُوٌّ لِي إِلَّا رَبَّ الْعَالَمِينَ ﴾ الشعراء: ٦٩ – ٧٧

*And rehearse to them Abraham's story. Behold, he said to his father and his people: 'What worship ye?' They said: 'We worship idols, and we remain constantly in attendance on them.' He said: 'Do they listen to you when you call (on them), or do you good or harm?' They said: 'Nay, but we found our fathers doing thus (what we do).' He said: 'Do you then see whom you have been worshipping - you and your fathers before you?- For they are enemies to me; not so the Lord and Cherisher of the Worlds.' [Ash Shu'ara', 26: 69-77].*

"When the people of prophet Ibrahim (peace be on him) told him that they worshipped idols (and constantly remained in attendance on them), he asked them if they, that is the persons after whom those idols were named, listened to them and responded to their supplications, because the subject plural pronoun in the word he used *(yasma'una kum)* refers to people. Otherwise, he would have used the pronoun denoting things *(tasma'ukum)*. Then he asked them if they really knew what they worshipped, telling them that 'they' (i.e. whoever they worshipped) were all an enemy to him except the Lord of the Worlds. In this statement, the prophet Ibrahim was clearly referring to the idols and those whose names they carried. In the above verse, prophet Ibrahim uses the pronoun *'hum'* (they) which is used for rational beings. If he had only meant the idols made of stone, he would have opted for the plural pronoun *'ha'*, which is used to refer to inanimate objects.

"It is clear, therefore, that in verses revolving around the same narrative, the Qur'an uses both pronouns – *'man'* (who) and *'ma'* (what) – to refer to the gods worshipped by polytheists. The reason for this, as I have already explained, is that when worshipping one saint, the earlier polytheists in fact worshipped several gods, including the idol or tomb they built for that saint or even the coverings of the tomb, in addition to the saint's gods.

"From our discussion of the reasons why Allah described these polytheists as worshippers of gods, idols, and images, and as people who associated partners with Him, it should be obvious that all these evils emanated from worshipping dead saints; it should also be clear that the polytheists' *shirk* could be ascribed to their fascination with and reverence for devout people.

"The use of different terms to refer to what polytheists worshipped is attributable to different reasons; the referent in all cases is one and the same thing. Commenting on these reasons, Al-Wakil writes:

'Those worshipped by them (the earlier polytheists) are described as *auliya'* (protectors or supporters) because they sought their support and protection through supplications or otherwise; this was the original term used to refer to them. They are also described as 'partners' because the polytheists worshipped them besides Allah as though they were His partners in this respect. In other contexts, they are labelled as 'gods' because the polytheists deified them in the full sense of the word: they worshipped them and invoked their help and protection. Likewise, they are termed 'idols' or 'statues' given their concrete or visible form, or whatever the polytheists made in the name of the saint they worshipped. The object of their worship is also described in the Qur'an as *'taghut'* since it led them astray and they in turn misled others, or 'the devil' since it seduced them into worshipping whatever they worshipped besides Allah:

﴿ إن يَدْعُونَ مِن دُونِهِ إلا إنَاثاً وَإن يَدْعُونَ إلا شَيْطَاناً مَريداً ﴾ النساء: ١١٧

*(The pagans), leaving Him, call but female (deities): they call upon but Satan the persistent rebel! [An-Nisa', 4: 117].*

'This verse describes what the polytheists worshipped both as 'female' deities and as 'Satan'.

'The friend of Allah, prophet Ibrahim (peace be on him), is reported by the Qur'an to have said to his father:

﴿ يَا أَبَتِ لا تَعْبُدِ الشَّيْطانَ ... ﴾ مريم: ٤٤

*O my father, serve not Satan ... [Maryam, 19: 44].*

'The objects worshipped by the earlier polytheists are occasionally referred to as *'zann'* (conjecture), since they thought them capable of bringing benefit or averting harm, or as *'hawa'* (caprice) since they were under the sway of their whims.

﴿ ... وَمَا يَتَّبِعُ الذِينَ يَدْعُونَ مِن دُونِ اللهِ شُرَكَاءَ إن يَتَّبِعُون إلَّا الظَّنَّ وَإن هُم إلا يَخْرُصُونَ ﴾ يونس: ٦٦

*... What do they follow who worship as His 'partners' other than Allah? They follow nothing but fancy, and they do nothing but lie. [Yunus, 10: 66].*

﴿ ... إِن يَتَّبِعُونَ إِلَّا الظَّنَّ وَمَا تَهْوَى الأَنفُسُ وَلَقَدْ جَاءَهُم مِن رَبِّهُمُ الهُدَى ﴾ النجم: ٢٣

*... They follow nothing but conjecture and what their own souls desire! Even though there has come to them Guidance from their Lord! [An Najm, 53: 23].*

﴿ أَفَرَأَيْتَ مَن اتَّخَذَ إِلَهَهُ هَوَاهُ وَأَضَلَّهُ اللهُ عَلَى عِلْمٍ ... ﴾ الجاثية: ٢٣

*Then have you considered the case of one who takes as his god his own desire? Allah has, knowing (him as such), left him astray ... [Al-Jathiya, 45: 23].*

'Their gods are also sometimes described as mere 'names' which have no referents given the fact that the polytheists considered them to be their protectors and intercessors, when Allah alone is the Protector, and all powers of intercession rest with Him only:

﴿ مَا تَعْبُدُونَ مِن دُونِهِ إِلَّا أَسْمَاءً سَمَّيْتُمُوهَا أَنتُم وَءَابَاؤُكُم مَا أَنزَلَ اللهُ بِهَا مِن سُلْطَانٍ ... ﴾ يوسف: ٤٠

*If not Him, you worship nothing but names which you have named, you and your fathers, for which Allah has sent you no authority. [Yusuf, 12: 40].'*

"You should not be deceived by the multitude of attributes used by polytheists as they all point to one and the same thing: an entity that is worshipped besides Allah. Nor should you be taken in by the variety of terms used since they all denote the same reality. The actions of present-day polytheists cannot be justified by the fallacy that their counterparts in the days of *jahiliyah* committed *shirk* through worshipping idols and calling them gods, whereas they only turn to saintly people. The truth is crystal clear in the light of the Qur'an which has dispelled the darkness of falsehood.